AWESOME OS

FISHING BIRDS OF THE WORLD

DONNA LOVE

Illustrated by Joyce Mihran Turley

"OSPREYPHABET" letters by Donna Love

Mountain Press Publishing
Missoula, Montana
2006

Library of Congress Cataloging-in-Publication Data

Love, Donna, 1956–
Awesome ospreys : fishing birds of the world / Donna Love ; illustrated by Joyce Mihran Turley.—1st ed.
p. cm.
ISBN 0-87842-512-8 (pbk. : alk. paper)
1. Osprey—Juvenile literature. I. Title.
QL696.F36L68 2005
598.9′3—dc22
2005028404

PRINTED IN HONG KONG BY MANTEC PRODUCTION COMPANY

Mountain Press Publishing Company
P.O. Box 2399, Missoula, MT 59806
406-728-1900

For my father, John Schuerch, who was the most awesome salmon fisherman the Nestucca River in Oregon ever knew, and for my mother, Nina, who loved birds. —DONNA

For my dad, Ted, who gave me my first drawing lessons, and my mother Hermine, who treasured books and would have been thrilled to see my published artwork. —JOYCE

ACKNOWLEDGMENTS

I would like to thank Dr. Alan F. Poole, editor of *The Birds of North America Online* at the Cornell Lab of Ornithology, for sharing his extensive knowledge of ospreys with us; Dr. Erick Greene, associate dean of Biological Sciences at the University of Montana, for his enthusiasm for our book; Joyce Turley, again, for her colorful and imaginative illustrations; editor Lynn Purl for her excellent assistance; and the staff of Mountain Press for their dedicated attention to detail. Finally, and always, I would like to thank the teachers and students of Seeley Lake Elementary School for putting up with all of my "projects." I enjoy learning from you. —DONNA

I am very appreciative of the opportunity to work with Donna Love on our second book together. Donna's lively manuscript provided inspiration for my images, and she offered numerous resources and technical guidance as my illustrations took shape. I am also grateful to have worked again with editor Lynn Purl, who made the whole project come together with her enthusiasm and expertise. —JOYCE

WHAT BIRD builds its large, highly visible nest at the top of a tall tree, eats fish that it catches underwater with its feet, and is known by people all over the world? An osprey!

An osprey is a large, eaglelike, fish-eating bird. It lives near water, where it builds its large nest out of heavy sticks at the top of a tree or other high place. To find food, an osprey soars high above the water watching for fish below. When it spots its prey, it drops like lightning. Landing with a splash, it stretches its long legs deep underwater to grasp the fish in its talons. Then, with a mighty flap of its wings, it lifts its dinner skyward. Ospreys live on every continent in the world except Antarctica, so people all over the world recognize this remarkable bird. How can an osprey build such a large nest, catch fish underwater with its feet, and live in so many places? To find out, let's explore this awesome fishing bird of the world.

RAPTOR CAPTURE

An osprey (AH-spree or AH-spray) is a **predator**, an animal that hunts and eats other animals. Its **prey**, what it eats, is mostly fish, but occasionally it will also eat other **aquatic**, or water, animals such as frogs, turtles, water snakes, and young alligators. Sometimes an osprey feeds on small animals that swim in the water, like muskrats and minks. Only rarely will an osprey catch a small animal on land, such as a squirrel or a mouse.

An osprey is also a **raptor**, or bird of prey, like an eagle or a hawk. A raptor uses keen eyesight to find its prey, sharp **talons** (the long claws on the end of its toes) to capture its prey, and a hooked beak to tear off bites of food.

FISH HAWK

Sometimes called a fish hawk, sea hawk, or fish eagle, an osprey is in the same scientific **order**, or division, of birds as hawks and eagles, Falconiformes (fal-coh-nih-FOR-meez), from the Latin for "sickle-shaped," for the birds' curved talons. However, an osprey has some physical traits that differ from an eagle's or hawk's, so scientists have traditionally put ospreys in a **family**, or group, of their own, Pandionidae (pan-die-AH-nih-dee).

There is only one species of osprey in the world, although there are several regional subspecies (see page 56), so all ospreys have the scientific name *Pandion haliaetus* (pan-DIE-on hal-ih-ay-EE-tus). They are the only members of their genus, whose name comes from Pandion, a mythological Greek king of Athens whose two daughters were turned into birds. The species name, *haliaetus*, is Latin for sea eagle. The common name, osprey, is from *ossifragus*, a Latin word meaning "bone breaker," referring to the strong grip of its talons. Ancient Romans called the osprey *sanqualis*, the "life-giving eagle." In Scotland, its Gaelic name, *lasgair*, means fisherman. In Mexico, its Spanish name, *aquila pescador* (ah-KEE-lah pes-kah-DOR), means "fisherman eagle."

OSPREY ODYSSEY

Osprey **fossils**, the bones and other remains of ancient animal life, show that ospreys have been on earth for 13 million years. An osprey from the past was smaller, but had a similar **range**, the places where it lives, as today.

People have long admired the osprey's fishing skills and strength, incorporating ospreys into their cultures. Ancient Greeks thought ospreys could predict lightning. Asian emperors had osprey pictures woven into palace tapestries. In South America, Native people used osprey feathers and bones in ceremonies to guarantee fishing success. In Canada, a Northwest Coast Indian legend tells of a marriage between an osprey and a whale that created the orca whale. An orca is actually a large black-and-white dolphin that jumps out of the water like a bird in flight and has a cry that sounds like an osprey's.

For many years, the Canadian ten-dollar bill had the picture of an osprey on it. More recently, in 1994, the osprey was named the provincial bird of Nova Scotia. Today, ospreys are still so highly thought of that some sports teams call themselves the Osprey and use an osprey for their mascot.

MISTAKEN IDENTITY

An osprey is a large bird that stands two feet tall and weighs up to four and a half pounds. An osprey's six-foot **wingspan**, or wingspread, is so large it is sometimes mistaken for an eagle, but an osprey's wing is narrower and curves backward at its wrist, like the wing of a gull. Unlike an eagle's wing, which is flat, an osprey's wing curves up in the middle. This curve provides the **lift**, or upward force, the osprey needs to rise out of the water with a large fish. In contrast to the eagle's, an osprey's forehead is smooth. Ospreys don't fly through trees and tall grass to catch their prey, so they don't need the bony ridge above their eyes that eagles have for protection.

An osprey's **field mark**, a trait used to identify an animal in the wild, is the dark **carpal**, or wrist, patch on the underside of each wing. The dark spot comes in handy when the bird is hunting. From a distance the dark spots look like two small birds dipping and soaring rather than one large bird about to strike.

ACTIVITY

To understand the crook or bend in an osprey's wing pretend that your arms are wings and hold them out from your sides. Bend your elbows slightly and turn your palms to face backwards. The curve you just formed, from your shoulder to wrist, matches the curve of an osprey's wing. Now imagine that your fingers have long flight feathers attached. Beneath your wrist is the carpal patch, the spot on an osprey's wing that is covered with dark feathers.

gull
osprey
eagle

HIDDEN HUNTER

An osprey wears light feathers on the underside of its body and dark feathers on top. The white feathers on its chest look like the light colors of the sky to its prey, fish swimming below. The dark colors **camouflage**, or hide, the osprey from its predators, large owls that attack from above. The brown and white **barred**, or evenly striped, feathers on the underside of an osprey's wings and tail help hide its shape in flight. To camouflage its head, an osprey wears dark spots on top, and a dark stripe through its eye area, like wraparound sunglasses. This eye stripe, called a **malar** (MAY-ler) stripe, may reduce sun glare, like the black grease used under the eyes by football players. An adult osprey's eyes are yellow. Its brown, hooked beak, its gray legs and feet, and its black talons don't reflect sunlight, so there's no glare to give away its position.

Unlike many birds, male and female ospreys dress alike, so it is hard to tell them apart. A female osprey is slightly larger, and usually wears a darker **necklace**, or band of speckles, across her white chest that helps her hide while nesting.

ALL-WEATHER FEATHERS

Do you like to play outside? An osprey spends its whole life outside. In its high nest and on its tall **perch**, or roost, the osprey is very exposed to the weather. On rainy days firm, stiff, slightly oily **contour**, or outer, feathers repel water to keep the bird dry. On cold days an osprey's **down**, the soft, fluffy inner feathers, helps keep its body warm.

An osprey **molts**, or replaces its feathers, slowly over the course of two years. It loses its **flight feathers**, the long, stiff feathers on the ends of its wings, at different times, so it is never missing two feathers next to each other, since that big a gap would interfere with flying. Just before **migration**, the regular movement of an animal from its summer home to its winter home, an osprey stops losing flight feathers, allowing the bird to fly its best while it migrates.

BIRDBATH

Ospreys need clean feathers to be able to fly and hunt, so they take good care of their **plumage**, or feathers. To wash itself, an osprey wades breast-deep into shallow water, puts its head underwater, and beats its wings. Then it shakes the excess water from its wings and flies to a sunny perch, where it may hold its wings out to dry like laundry hanging on a clothesline. The only time an osprey doesn't bathe as regularly is when the female **incubates**, or sits on, eggs in the nest to keep them warm. She will sneak in an occasional bath when the male brings fish back to the nest and sits on the eggs for her.

In addition to washing its feathers, an osprey **preens**, or grooms its plumage, several times a day by running each large feather through its closed bill. After feeding, an osprey may wipe its beak on a branch, or flick away fish scales by shaking its head back and forth. To clean its feet it flies low over the surface of the water and drags them through the water. It may also do this to cool itself on a hot day.

SKYDIVER

Would you like to skydive? An osprey's **skeleton**, or bone structure, is made for skydiving. To reduce **drag**, or wind resistance, an osprey's head is small. Its short neck helps reduce body weight. Strong chest muscles attached to an osprey's extra-large breastbone provide the power for its long wings to lift and carry a heavy fish. As with other birds, a fused, or solid, backbone provides a sturdy platform for its wings to push against.

An osprey's leg attaches far back on its body so its leg doesn't get in the way of its wing. Its thighbone is held close to its body inside the skin covering the body cavity. Its leg comes out of its body cavity below its knee. A long, slender calf bone allows the osprey to reach deep underwater. Below the calf bone, what looks like a backward-facing knee is really the bird's ankle. The elevated ankle gives the bird spring during takeoff and landing. Like other birds, the osprey has only one long foot bone. The osprey doesn't stand on its heels like humans do; it stands on its toes. Flexible toes allow the bird to hold on to a craggy perch or carry a heavy fish.

FISH GRIP

Like oversize socks, an osprey wears loose skin on its large feet so it can stretch its toes deep underwater. Barbed scales on the undersides of its feet, called **spicules** (SPICK-yules), help it hold on to slippery fish. An osprey has four long, movable toes on each foot, and it is the only raptor with toes all the same length. Three of its toes are in front and one is in back. Like an owl, an osprey can rotate the outside toe to the back, so it can hold a fish with two toes on one side of the fish and two on the other side to form a strong grip.

On the ends of its toes the osprey has long, sharp, deeply curved talons. It is the only diurnal raptor (a raptor active during the daytime) to have talons the same length as its toes; it is also the only raptor whose talons are completely round from base to tip. These long, round talons are perfect for piercing the tough skin of a fish. An osprey's talons are made of **keratin**, the same substance as your fingernails. If part of a talon breaks off it will slowly grow back.

ACTIVITY

To understand which osprey toe moves to the back, hold your hands in front of you, palms down. If you were an osprey, your little finger, the one on the outside of your hand, could swing around to help your thumb pick up an object.

WIND WALKER

If you could fly, would you ever walk? An osprey rarely walks. Its large talons get in the way. In its nest it curls its talons in and moves slowly so it doesn't harm its eggs or chicks.

An osprey is a strong flier, flying with a slightly circular or rowing motion. Quick, shallow wing beats, the up-and-down movement of a bird's wings, make it look like it flies faster, but an osprey only flies as fast as a car driving in town, about twenty-five miles per hour. An osprey flaps its whole wing when it flies, but the curve in its wing makes it appear that only the outer part of the wing, from the elbow out, moves.

An osprey is an **active flier**, flapping its wings more often than holding them still, but it can soar or glide for a short time. An osprey likes to soar on **thermals**, natural currents of warm air rising high above the earth, which carry the bird high into the sky.

ACTIVITY

To see what it is like to fly like an osprey, hold your arms slightly above your head and flap your arms, but when you flap, only bring your arms down as far as your shoulders before quickly raising them again. Now you are flying like an osprey.

HEALTHY HABITATS

Would you rather live in the mountains or near the ocean? An osprey can catch fish in freshwater or saltwater, so an osprey can live far from the ocean or right at the beach. All an osprey needs is fish to eat, water that isn't frozen, and a safe place to perch and nest. A river, lake, marsh, pond, or reservoir would each be a good freshwater osprey **habitat**, or the type of place where it lives best. A **coastal estuary**, which is a large, partly enclosed area where a freshwater stream meets the saltwater ocean, is also good osprey habitat.

So many places make good osprey habitat that ospreys live on every continent in the world except Antarctica, where even the summers are too cold. Ospreys can live in such a variety of **climates**, or average weather conditions, that they can be seen flying over a chilly Alaskan lake or sitting in a mangrove tree in sunny Florida. They can live in so many places that **ornithologists**, scientists who study birds, call the osprey the Citizen of the World.

FLY-FISHING

Shallow, clear, slow-moving water makes good **fishing territory**, the place where an osprey likes to fish. On the ocean, an osprey hunts in deep water where a **school**, or group, of fish gather near the surface. An osprey knows what to look for. It has in mind a **search image**, the pattern of a group of fish, which it learned while fishing with its parents.

An osprey hunts by sitting on a perch near its fishing territory, or by slowly flying in circles above it. It can spot a fish two hundred feet away. On the ocean the osprey may fly higher to find a school of fish, then drop lower for the catch. An osprey usually hunts in the morning and late afternoon, but it may hunt at other times. On the ocean an osprey hunts most at **mid tide**, halfway between low tide and high tide, no matter which direction the water is flowing. An osprey can fish in most weather, but if it is too windy it can't fly well. On a nice day it generally takes the osprey less than half an hour to make a catch, snagging a fish in one out of three tries.

CATCH OF THE DAY

Can you imagine eating nothing but fish for every meal? Fish provide all the **nutrients**, or food, an osprey needs, including liquid, although on a hot day an osprey may sip water from the shore.

An osprey will eat any kind of live fish, but it mostly catches **forage**, or bottom-feeding, fish that live in shallow water. A forage fish is slower and has its attention focused downward at its food instead of up where the osprey is, so it is an easier fish to catch. However, an osprey eats whatever fish is plentiful at the time. On the ocean an osprey may catch forage fish such as flounder, or a schooling fish such as herring. In fresh water, an osprey may catch suckers, catfish, or perch. When an osprey spots its prey it **hovers**, or flies in one place, fanning its wings. An osprey is the only raptor that can hover while it decides the best angle of attack. A steep dive will catch a fish up to three feet underwater. A shallow dive will catch a fish near the surface.

ACTIVITY

Have you ever skipped a rock across the surface of the water? The rock goes into the water at a shallow or low angle and glides across the surface. This is how an osprey catches fish in shallow water. If an osprey wants to catch a fish in deep water it doesn't glide over the surface of the water; it drops straight down, like a rock dropped into water does.

ON TARGET

During a dive an osprey drops out of the sky headfirst, its wings slightly folded, legs trailing behind. A dive may be made in stairstep stages or it may be a drop of up to seventy feet, the height of a seven-story building. Dropping at great speeds, sometimes up to forty miles per hour, the bird makes adjustments with its tail to direct it to its prey. An osprey understands the effects of underwater **light refraction**, the bend in a ray of light as it goes underwater, so an osprey can accurately aim for its prey, even if the fish isn't exactly where it looks like it is.

Like your eyes, an osprey's eyes face forward, so each eye sees an overlapping view of what the other eye sees. This is called **binocular vision**. This gives an osprey good **depth perception**, the ability to correctly judge the distance to an object. An osprey can see five times more clearly than people can, so it easily spots its prey. Have you seen pilots and swimmers wearing goggles? The osprey carries its own goggles to protect its eyes. The osprey closes the **nictitating membrane**, a thin layer of clear tissue like an inner eyelid, over its eye in flight to keep the eye moist. During a dive the membrane protects the eye when the osprey hits the water.

ACTIVITY

To understand the effects of underwater light refraction, fill a bowl or dishpan with water. Place a small object such as a rock or coin in the water. Now reach underwater and try to put one finger on the object. Whoa! This is hard to do. After a few tries your brain makes the adjustment and you can place your finger on the object.

FLY CATCH

When the diving osprey gets close to the water it throws its feet forward and hits the water with a big splash. An osprey is the only raptor that plunges feet first under the water for its food, and it is the only raptor with nose flaps that close so it can go completely under the surface. Featherless lower legs and small, compact feathers around its knees allow its legs to slide underwater quickly. An osprey can reach up to three feet underwater. When an osprey feels its prey wiggle beneath its foot, it clamps its talons shut faster than you can say "osprey!"

After making the catch, the osprey may struggle with its prey for a moment at the water's surface. When it has the fish gripped firmly in its talons, the osprey uses its strong chest muscles to flap its wings, lifting itself and the fish out of the water.

DO THE TWIST

An osprey can catch a fish that weighs more than a pound, one-third its own bodyweight. The osprey's lightweight body, its long wingspan, and the curve of its wing help it lift and carry a large fish. However, it isn't easy for an osprey to fly with wet wings. To get rid of excess water, an osprey twists its body from head to tail like a wet dog shaking after a bath.

After shaking the water from its wings, an osprey speeds nestward with its catch. It can't waste time. An osprey's perch or nest can be several miles from its fishing territory, so it may have to fly a long way to get home. If its prey is small, the osprey carries it in one foot. The osprey has a distinctive way of carrying larger fish: to streamline its load for flight, the osprey turns the fish headfirst and clutches it with both feet, one foot in front of the other along the fish's backbone.

ACTIVITY

To see what it is like to lift a heavy fish out of the water, fill a bowl or dishpan with water. Place a rock or other heavy object underwater. Move the rock around without taking it out of the water. It feels light and moves easily. Now pull the rock out of the water. As soon as it clears the surface it feels heavy, so you have to work harder to lift it. An osprey has to work hard, too. An osprey lifting a one-pound fish is like a sixty-pound person lifting twenty pounds.

DINING OUT

After the catch, an osprey carries its prey to its perch and eats its meal. The osprey tears the fish apart with its sharp, hooked beak, starting with the head.

An osprey only eats fresh food, so it doesn't **cache** (pronounced kash), or store, its food the way some animals do. It eats all it can at the time of the catch and leaves the rest. Its **crop**, a pouch in its throat, stores food waiting to go to its stomach. This allows the osprey to eat more food and wait longer between meals. An osprey eats every part of the fish. Like other birds, the osprey has a **gizzard**, a strong, muscular part of the stomach that grinds hard parts of food into small pieces. In its stomach the hardest pieces of food and fish scales are packed into a **pellet**, a small mass of undigested food, which the osprey occasionally spits out. Most of what an osprey eats is **digestible**, or able to be processed by its body, so it does not produce pellets very often.

SKY DANCE

Osprey pairs live apart in winter, but in the spring they usually return to the same nest where they raised chicks the previous year. The male generally arrives first. If one in the pair doesn't return, the remaining bird will likely pick a new mate. During **courtship**, when the birds pick a mate, the male calls to the female and flies over the nest carrying a fish or nest material to prove he is a strong flier and good provider. His **sky dance** may last ten minutes. If the female likes him she will let him land beside her. After mating, the male guards her wherever she goes and provides all her food, a behavior known as **courtship feeding**.

Nest building begins right away. Nests are usually built in the open on a tall tree or cliff overlooking an osprey's fishing territory. If surrounded by water the nest doesn't have to be as high. On a predator-free island an osprey pair may even nest on the ground. When food is abundant an osprey might nest in a **colony**, or group, near other ospreys. A breeding pair may share its fishing territory with other ospreys, but not its nest.

CREAMING EAGLE

An osprey can communicate well with its mate and other ospreys. Its **guard call**, used to protect its nest, is a series of loud, slow whistles. If an osprey feels threatened it uses a **scream call**, a squeal also used by the male during courtship. Its **alarm call**, a screech, is sounded when a predator or disturbance comes close to its nest. This call is given most often by the female. The female relies on the male for food while she is nesting and caring for the chicks, so she also has a **solicitation call**, a chirp that lets her mate know when she is hungry. An osprey can hear well. Its ears are small openings covered by feathers on the sides of its head.

An osprey at rest sits upright. If it feels threatened it will stand up, stretch its neck and hold its wings out from its sides. If the danger gets too close, the osprey shakes its wings, spreads its tail, and calls its guard or scream call. If the danger comes even closer the osprey may fly at the intruder and try to strike it in the air with its talons.

TREE HOUSE

To build its nest the male osprey gathers sticks and the female arranges them. Large sticks make up the base of the nest, and smaller sticks are placed on top. Then the nest is lined with grass, seaweed, and other fine material that keep the eggs from falling into the cracks. An osprey uses the same nest year after year, adding on to it. An older nest can weigh up to one thousand pounds. Smaller birds might nest in the outer branches of a large osprey nest. The osprey doesn't harm the little birds and their nest is protected when an osprey protects its own family.

When the nest is complete, the female lays up to four large, chestnut-speckled eggs. She will incubate the eggs to keep them warm for thirty-eight to forty-two days, staying with them day and night to protect them from owls, ravens, and raccoons. The male guards the female and provides her food. He may incubate the eggs while she eats. Both parents have a **brood patch**, a patch of bare skin on their bellies that they place over the eggs to keep them warm.

HIGH-RISE APARTMENT

Osprey chicks usually hatch one to two days apart. Nests near the ocean usually have the largest **broods**, or number of chicks. Inland, where fish are less abundant, only one chick may survive. If a nest fails, the pair may build a **frustration nest** while they are upset at the loss. Eggs are rarely laid in this new nest, but it will be ready for the next year. The osprey pair may use it, or a new pair might move in.

A newly hatched chick is about the size of a plum and is covered in pale tan down; about ten days later brown and yellow striped down comes in, helping camouflage it in the nest. The chick is helpless at first, and its orange eyes are almost blind. The female protects the chick from predators, storms, and hot sun. The male provides food, delivering fish up to eight times a day. After catching a fish, he flies to his perch and eats part of it himself. Then he takes the rest to the female and she feeds small bites to the chick. When the chick is full, she eats what remains, including the fins and tail.

LIFTOFF

By nine weeks an oprey chick has grown its **juvenile** feathers, the feathers an immature bird has until it reaches adulthood. These include the flight feathers that it will wear for the first two years of its life. These feathers have light-colored tips so it is easy to tell a young bird from its parents. To learn to fly the chick holds its wings open to feel the wind beneath them. One day the wind may simply lift the chick out of the nest. Its first flights are short. As its skills improve the chick will leave the nest for the day and return at night.

Osprey parents feed the chick for three months. Once the chick can fly, its parents feed it less to encourage it to take care of itself. A chick that has **fledged**, or learned to fly, may land on a younger chick's nest and be fed a meal or two by its temporarily adopted parents. By **instinct**, a trait it is born with, the chick begins to dive after fish. After a few days a chick can feed itself, but it takes months before it learns to hunt as well as its parents can.

WINTER BREAK

By autumn, a chick is ready to migrate. It migrates alone, following major **flyways**, the migration routes of other birds. An osprey can fly for three days without stopping, so it can fly over large bodies of water or deserts. An osprey may stop near water to rest and feed. It may rest several days before moving on.

The ospreys that fly the farthest north in summer often fly the farthest south in winter. Some ospreys migrate 4,000 miles from the Northern Hemisphere to the Southern Hemisphere. Imagine having a summer home in a Canadian forest and taking an incredible journey every year to live among the mangroves of Brazil, where it will also be summer when you arrive. Ospreys that live where it is warm all year don't migrate, but they do take a break from their mates and nests.

In winter an osprey spends its time alone or, if food is abundant, may roost with other ospreys. An osprey can live to be twenty years old. For the first two years a chick remains at its winter home. Then it returns to its **natal**, or birth, nest. A young male doesn't nest far from home, but a young female may travel up to three hundred miles to find a mate. By the age of five an osprey will likely pick a mate and raise chicks of its own.

WEATHERING THE STORM

Only a few things in nature harm an osprey. Hurricanes or lightning may strike its nest. It may die from extreme heat or extreme cold, or from starvation if it can't catch enough fish.

People can cause other problems. In the past, fishermen who felt ospreys ate too many fish killed many of the birds. When egg collecting became popular for amateur or untrained naturalists, osprey nests were raided for their pretty eggs. Beaver trapping destroyed beaver ponds. The pesticide **DDT**, a chemical used in the United States until the 1970s to kill insects, caused females to lay soft-shelled eggs that broke before they could hatch. Like many raptors, ospreys were highly affected because their prey ate contaminated insects, so the chemicals **biomagnified**, or built up in the birds' bodies.

Shoreline development, water pollution, the draining of wetlands, and excessive logging can destroy osprey habitat. Too many boats on an osprey's fishing territory can cause ospreys to move. An osprey can get caught in commercial fishing nets or tangled in fishing line and drown. It can collide with power lines or motor vehicles. It may become snared in rope or other items it carries to its nest; old shoes, dolls, and even hula-hoops have been found woven into nests.

ACTIVITY

To show how chemicals biomagnify in the body of a predator, place twenty small paper cups, representing DDT, inside ten medium paper cups representing insects. Then place the ten medium paper cups inside two larger cups, representing fish. Finally, place the two large paper cups, filled with all the other paper cups, inside one large cup, representing an osprey. The large cup now contains all the DDT that was first eaten by the insects. This is how harmful chemicals build to a dangerous level in fish-eating birds like ospreys.

FIRST AID

Today, many people help ospreys. **Wildlife biologists**, people who study wild animals, may place a small transmitter on an osprey so it can be tracked by satellite to learn where it goes. **Fisheries biologists**, people who study fish, preserve fish populations and help ospreys in the process. Some countries have laws that ban harmful chemicals. Stiff wires or fake owls placed at the top of power poles keep ospreys from roosting there. Man-made nest platforms provide safe places for ospreys to nest. These are critical to the recovery of osprey populations in many areas. For example, ninety-seven percent of the more than 700 pairs nesting between New York City and Boston now use artificial platforms. Raccoon guards can be placed around nest trees or poles. Rope, string, and other harmful items can be removed from a nest in winter so the osprey has a safe nest to return to.

An osprey is a bird that can adapt to change. In some places, large cities have grown up around osprey nests. Some schools near osprey habitat have built nest platforms so students can learn about ospreys. Places where people respect animals' homes will probably always have ospreys. All an osprey needs is a safe place to perch and nest, a place to fish, and plenty of fish to eat.

OSPREY *(Pandion halieatus)*

An osprey is a large bird standing 21 to 25 inches tall. It has a wingspan of 6 feet. Males are slightly smaller than females. The osprey is dark brown on top and white underneath. The female wears a necklace of darker speckles across her white breast. An osprey's head is white with a dark, masklike stripe running through its eye area and across its cheek. Its eyes are yellow and its bill and talons are black. An immature osprey wears white tips on the ends of its brown feathers, and its eyes are orange.

An osprey lives near a body of water, such as a river, lake, or ocean. It hunts alone, feeding mostly on live fish that it catches with its feet. The osprey builds a bulky stick nest, typically high above the ground at the top of a tall tree, often using the same nest over and over. Up to four chestnut-speckled eggs incubate for thirty-eight to forty-two days. The chicks are fed by the parents for three months. The chicks fledge at nine weeks. An osprey can live to be twenty years old.

Four subspecies of osprey live in the world. Each has its own range.

Pandion haliaetus leucocephalus (loo-ko-SEF-uh-lus) lives in Australia and the southwest Pacific Islands. In winter this subspecies doesn't migrate far from its summer home. Ospreys in Australia don't migrate out of Australia.

P.h. haliaetus lives in Europe, Northwest Africa, and Northern Asia. It migrates further than other subspecies, flying over 4,000 miles to winter in Africa, India, or the East Indies. A few live year-round near the Mediterranean Sea.

P.h. ridgwayi (RIJ-way-eye) lives in the Caribbean from the Bahamas to Belize, and along the coast of southeast Mexico. In winter it doesn't migrate far from its summer home

P.h. carolinensis nests in North America and flies up to 3,000 miles to spend its winters in Central and South America.

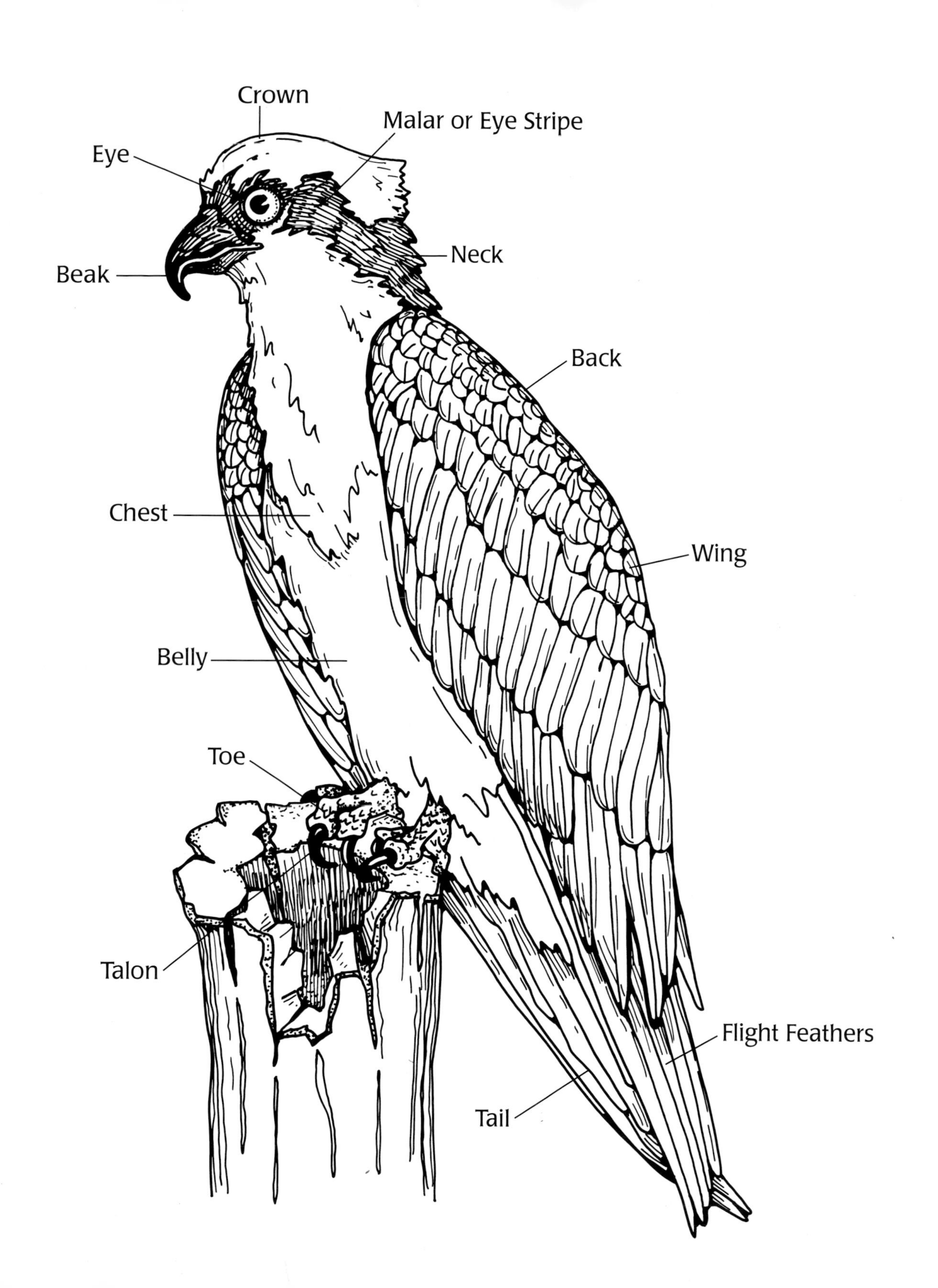
Crown
Malar or Eye Stripe
Eye
Neck
Beak
Back
Chest
Wing
Belly
Toe
Talon
Flight Feathers
Tail

OSPREY RESOURCE LIST

Web Sites

These are some of the organizations that help care for ospreys. Some of the sites are managed by the government, some by an organization, and a few by volunteers.

California Institute for Wildlife Studies
www.iws.org
Santa Catalina Island, California, lost its ospreys. Find out how the island got them back. Click on "species," then "birds," and go to osprey. To view a nest built low over water, scroll down the page.

Cornell Lab of Ornithology
www.birds.cornell.edu/programs/AllAboutBirds/BirdGuide/
You can listen to an osprey's call on this site, and see lots of detailed information and photographs.

Friends of Blackwater
www.friendsofblackwater.org
At this site click on Site Map and scroll down to find the Osprey Cam. Here you can see osprey Web cams or take an osprey quiz. Teachers will like the 36-page "Project Osprey Curriculum: The Return of the Fish Hawk," with information and activities to help students learn about the needs of ospreys.

International Osprey Foundation
www.ospreys.com
Go to this site to find three live Webcams, osprey movies, sounds, and more.

Martha's Vineyard Osprey Pages
Department of Biology, UNC Charlotte
http://www.bioweb.uncc.edu/bierregaard/ospreys.htm
Here you can follow the journeys of individual ospreys as their migrations are tracked via satellite. The site includes bird biographies, maps, photos, and lots of exciting information.

New York Wild
www.newyorkwild.org/osprey/osprey.htm
See live and recorded video of ospreys nesting at Montezuma National Wildlife Refuge in New York state.

Oriental Bird Club
www.orientialbirdimages.org
Can ospreys really live all over the world? Search for "osprey" and see photographs from many countries, including Malaysia, Africa, India, Australia, and Indonesia.

Osprey page of Ruud Kampf of the Netherlands
www.rekel.nl/visarenden
Can an osprey catch two fish at the same time? Go to this site and scroll down to see a remarkable photograph that answers this question.

Royal Society for the Protection of Birds
www.rspb.org.uk
Find out how folks in the United Kingdom care for ospreys in England, Scotland, and Ireland.

Rutlands Wildlife Trust
www.ospreys.org.uk
Read about the reintroduction of ospreys to central England and see amazing photos, like a pair of ospreys carrying a swordfish together, a nest on a cactus, and more. A kids' quiz is also offered here.

Tweed Valley Wildlife Carers, New South Wales, Australia
www.tvwc.org
What made Pierre the osprey sick? Click on "Featured Animals" and scroll down to read about this Australian bird's care and recovery.

University of Michigan Museum of Zoology Animal Diversity Web
http://animaldiversity.ummz.umich.edu/site/accounts/information/Pandion_haliaetus.html
Find detailed information, photos, maps, and a recording of an osprey call here.

USGS – Patuxent Bird Identification InfoCenter
www.mbr-pwrc.usgs.gov/id/framlst/i3640id.html
Check this site out to find a detailed species account of the North American osprey, complete with range map and identification tips.

Osprey Books

"Osprey: Pandion haliaetus." Alan F. Poole, Rob O. Bierregaard, and Mark S. Martell. In *The Birds of North America*, No. 683. (A. Poole and F. Gill, eds.). The Birds of North America, Inc., Philadelphia, PA, 2002.
For the serious student, this thirty-six page species account combines all the known research about the osprey into one compact report. Includes range map, graphs, and diagrams.

Ospreys. Roy Dennis. Colin Baxter Photography, Ltd., Great Britain, 1991.
Written by a well-known ornithologist from Scotland, this book takes a factual look at ospreys, describing the osprey's decline and recovery in Scotland and Europe. Includes large color photographs.

Ospreys: A Natural and Unnatural History. Alan F. Poole. Cambridge University Press, Cambridge and New York, 1989.
Written by one of the world's leading osprey researchers, this book takes a thorough, scientific, in-depth look at ospreys. Includes research and graphs.

Return of the Osprey: A Season of Flight and Wonder. David Gessner. The Ballantine Publishing Group, New York, 2001.
While taking time off to recover from an illness, this nature writer returns to his family's seashore home, lives on "osprey time," and learns many lessons from the osprey.

Osprey Books for Children

Orca's Song. Anne Cameron. Harbour Publishing, Madeira Park, BC, 1996.
This Northwest Coast Indian legend tells the story of an osprey and a whale that fall in love.

Ospreys. Dorothy Hinshaw Patent. Clarion Books, New York. 1993.
Learn about ospreys from an award-winning author and zoologist. Includes many color photographs.

Return of the Osprey. Patricia Mason. Harbour Publishing, Madeira Park, BC, 1999.
When Grandfather takes five-year-old Joseph to Maplewood Flats, ospreys abound. Will Joseph still find ospreys when he returns years later with his own young family?

INDEX

ABOUT THE AUTHOR

Donna Love lives in Seeley Lake, Montana, where her husband, Tim, is the district ranger for the Seeley Lake Ranger District on the Lolo National Forest. Donna's first book, ***Loons: Diving Birds of the North,*** was published by Mountain Press in 2003. She has continued her work with loons, but has added another specialty. While watching loons on the lake right outside her door she became fascinated by a pair of ospreys that built their nest, hatched their eggs, and raised their chicks within view of her home. Her observations led her to research and develop a children's program and slide show, "Awesome Ospreys," for use in grade schools and at public events. This program formed the basis of her new book. She is also an artist, adding the "ospreyphabet" letters to her growing portfolio of artwork.

ABOUT THE ILLUSTRATOR

In the early 1990s, Operation Osprey successfully reintroduced ospreys to Fort Collins, Colorado. Over ten years later, **Joyce Mihran Turley** has been able to observe nesting ospreys close to her home in the foothills of the Rocky Mountains. With a background in mathematics, she retired from engineering twenty years ago to spend time with her family and to pursue a career in illustration. Her unique perspective as an engineer, artist, and parent is reflected in much of her artwork, with scientifically accurate illustrations rendered in a lively palette. She has illustrated books on many topics, and especially enjoys illustrating nonfiction subjects for children. She previously collaborated with Donna Love on ***Loons: Diving Birds of the North.*** Joyce's work may be viewed at www.dixoncovedesign.com.